AF381596

MINDFULNESS

The secrets to inner peace and harmony

Written by Maïlys Charlier
In collaboration with Céline Faidherbe
Translated by Rebecca Neal

Health and Wellbeing 50MINUTES.com

MINDFULNESS   11

WHAT IS MINDFULNESS?   15

Mindfulness meditation

The positive effects of mindfulness

The different schools of mindfulness

The obstacles to mindfulness

Encouragements to mindfulness

MINDFULNESS MEDITATION   29

Preparing for mindfulness meditation

Mindfulness meditation techniques

Tips and tricks

INCORPORATING MINDFULNESS INTO YOUR EVERYDAY LIFE   39

Other techniques

FAQS   45

Is meditation absolutely necessary to achieve mindfulness?

How much time should I dedicate to practising mindfulness?

How can I use mindfulness to resolve conflicts?

What are the benefits of mindfulness?

What are the links between slow life and mindfulness?

Do I have to be an expert in spirituality to meditate?

What should I do when my thoughts get in the way of mindfulness?

MINDFULNESS

TECHNIQUES FOR LIVING IN THE MOMENT

- **Problem:** how can you use meditation or other techniques to achieve mindfulness?
- **Aims:** to learn to live in the moment and calm your thoughts thanks to a range of mindfulness techniques.
- **FAQs:**
  - Is meditation absolutely necessary to achieve mindfulness?
  - How much time should I dedicate to practising mindfulness?
  - How can I use mindfulness to resolve conflicts?
  - What are the benefits of mindfulness?
  - What are the links between slow life and mindfulness?
  - Do I have to be an expert in spirituality to meditate?
  - What should I do when my thoughts get in the way of mindfulness?

"Mindfulness" refers to a form of meditation derived from the teachings of Gautama Buddha (spiritual leader of Nepalese origin, c. 5th century BCE) which is characterised by an awareness of our own thoughts, actions and motivations in the present moment. It is a simple practice which involves bringing our attention back to the present, observing and focusing on the sensations we experience. It is closely linked to Buddhism and meditation, although it is present in a wide range of religions and traditions. It is used in the West as a way of treating stress and depression.

According to Svea and Arist von Hehn, the authors of the 2015 book *La Pleine Conscience. Apprendre à méditer au quotidien !* ("Mindfulness: Learn to Meditate Every Day!"), mental distraction is extremely common. Indeed, a 2010 Harvard University study revealed that our mind is wandering 50% of the time (Killingsworth and Gilbert, 2010).

This all means that we multitask, spend a lot of time thinking about the past and the future and struggle to live in the present. Unsurprisingly, our distractedness does not make us happy: the study also showed that a wandering mind leads to emotional fatigue.

The French psychiatrist Christophe André (born in 1956) defines mindfulness as "the attention we devote to our experience with no filter, no judgment and no expectations"[1] (2010). We can all achieve this state if we let ourselves be guided and learn while practising it.

In 50 minutes, this guide will show you how you can attain this state of mindfulness, the benefits it can bring you, and how you can practise it on a daily basis.

1. This quotation has been translated by 50Minutes.com.

WHAT IS MINDFULNESS?

MINDFULNESS MEDITATION

Mindfulness meditation involves focusing your attention on the present moment as often as possible, examining the thoughts and feelings you are experiencing and letting them wash over you without trying to control, judge or analyse them. It means halting the constant stream of thoughts which bombard us with self-criticism and judgment.

Whereas mindfulness is a mental state, mindfulness mediation is a technique to reach this state. The goal of mindfulness meditation is to switch off autopilot and start thinking about everything we are doing.

According to André, mindfulness mediation means "being fully aware of the moment and the feelings, thoughts and emotions that accompany it". This technique "encourages a mental state which protects against stress and depression"[1] (*ibid.*).

There are a number of common misconceptions about meditation which may leave us thinking that it requires immense self-discipline and long hours of intense reflection. However, there are different types of meditation, some of which are more demanding than others. Mindfulness meditation is a kind of contemplative meditation: it involves consciously observing ourselves, which does not require strenuous mental effort.

THE POSITIVE EFFECTS OF MINDFULNESS

According to André, mindfulness contributes to our wellbeing and happiness. Many scientific studies have drawn the same conclusions: mindfulness is good for us and contributes to lasting happiness, and on average people who practise mindfulness are happier than those who do not.

Mindfulness has a noticeable impact on our mood and emotional state. It leads to greater

---

1. This quotation has been translated by 50Minutes.com.

happiness, peace of mind, confidence and self-acceptance, and allows us to make the most of the present and better regulate our emotions. Mindfulness also teaches us to be patient and sharpens our memory.

Research carried out by Svea and Aristide von Hehn has shown that meditation also improves our overall health: it improves our relationship with our bodies as we are more aware of them, makes it easier to deal with our emotions and physical pain, strengthens our immune system, reduces our stress levels and makes it easier to manage stress. This means that mindfulness has a significant positive effect on our quality of life.

A number of scientific studies have suggested that mindfulness could even have beneficial effects for people suffering from certain illnesses such as heart problems, chronic pain, respiratory problems and skin conditions. The Canadian psychologist Michael Speca from the University of Calgary has carried out a study on cancer patients which showed that mindfulness improved their mood, reduced symptoms linked to stress and diminished fatigue.

THE DIFFERENT SCHOOLS OF MINDFULNESS

Mindfulness-Based Stress Reduction (MBSR)

MBSR was developed by the American scientist Jon Kabat-Zinn in 1975 and aims to use mindfulness to combat anxiety, stress and pain. It is a programme of exercises which combines traditional mindfulness practices and research on stress, and was originally developed to treat chronic pain and the symptoms of stress.

Mindfulness-Based Cognitive Therapy (MBCT)

Having witnessed the effectiveness of MBSR, the Canadian psychiatrist Zindel Segal developed Mindfulness-Based Cognitive Therapy (for Depression). He spent two years observing and analysing 160 people with depression and anxiety disorders. After two years of treatment using MBCT (a psychotherapy programme based on mindfulness which uses the same methods as cognitive behavioural therapy), the patients made similar progress as would be expected after two years on antidepressants, without the side effects of medication.

Dialectical Behaviour Therapy (DBT)

DBT is a form of cognitive behavioural therapy developed at the University of Washington by the behavioural psychologist Marsha Linehan. Linehan works primarily with cases of borderline personality disorder, a condition characterised by extreme emotional sensitivity which sees patients swing from euphoria to depression in the space of a moment. According to Linehan's work, regular zen meditation gives patients greater emotional awareness, which in turn enables them to better tolerate painful emotions.

The Vittoz method

The Vittoz method was developed by the Swiss doctor Roger Vittoz and allows patients to move past mental and behavioural habits and reflections linked to the past. The method involves regularly focusing your attention on the sensory experiences of the present moment.

Open Focus Therapy (OFT)

OFT was developed by the American psychologist Les Fehmi. It comprises a series of exercises to regulate our attention, with the aim of moving away from narrow-objective focus (focusing on an idea) and towards diffuse-immersed attention (remaining open to our surroundings).

THE OBSTACLES TO MINDFULNESS

In modern Western society, the pace of life is hectic and we are constantly working and doing more. Some of us are even working two jobs just to make ends meet. This pace of life means that our brains are working faster than before, which leaves us little time to relax and take care of ourselves.

This is why we often find ourselves thinking about the past or the future, but all this does is make us uneasy, as we cannot change the past or control the future. Consequently, all our thoughts about the past ("I should have acted differently", "The party last night was great", and so on) or the future ("What am I going to eat tonight?", "I'll never find anyone, I'm going to end up alone", and so on) can only cause nostalgia and suffering. Mindfulness, which encourages us to concentrate on the moment, can alleviate this emotional suffering.

It is a reflex: our thoughts are naturally prone to wandering. At some point we have all found ourselves distracted by our thoughts while reading a book, cooking or watching a film. For example, on Sunday evenings most of us are already thinking about Monday and the week ahead of us at work. We do not make the most of the end of the weekend and are already thinking: "The weekend is over. It's back to work tomorrow."

The moment when we regain control of our thoughts and start concentrating on the present again is a moment of mindfulness. Our wandering thoughts are constantly dragging us away from the present: when we are lost in these thoughts, we are either anticipating and planning the future, or remembering the past.

According to the psychologist Svea von Hehn and the founder of Teach First, Arist von Hehn, the obstacles to living in the present can be classified into three categories:

- Desire for the things we want to possess.
- Repulsion for things we do not want to have or things we do not want to happen to us.
- Ignorance, meaning the inability to distinguish the true nature of things from our interpretations of what other people think and the meaning of certain situations. Our belief that we understand the situation and know for certain what other people think may lead us away from the truth.

The various factors which are responsible for these attitudes affect all of us. These include the pace of life imposed by our culture and the latest developments in technology (it is difficult to live in the moment when every minute of our time is accounted for and our smartphones send us constant reminders and notifications), and evolutionary biology, as anticipating future events is a survival mechanism.

Ruth Baer of the University of Kentucky has developed the Mindfulness Attention Awareness Scale (MAAS) to measure our ability to reach mindfulness. The MAAS is a questionnaire that allows us to evaluate our attitude to mindfulness. The questions take the form of affirmations that focus on our ability to be present or absent and on whether or not we are distracted in our daily lives.

The individual must indicate whether each affirmation applies to them "almost always", "very frequently", "somewhat frequently", "somewhat infrequently", "very infrequently" or "almost never". At the end of the questionnaire, a points scale allows them to determine to what extent they are naturally in a mindful state. The questionnaire's affirmations include statements like "I forget a person's name almost as soon as I've been told it for the first time", "I do jobs or tasks automatically, without being aware of what I'm doing" and "I snack without being aware that I'm eating".

ENCOURAGEMENTS TO MINDFULNESS

There are a number of attitudes that can help us to attain a state of mindfulness. According to Jon Kabat-Zinn, who developed the MBSR method to reduce stress, there are seven attitudes we can cultivate to work towards mindfulness:

non-judging, patience, beginner's mind, trust, non-striving, acceptance and letting go. In the 1980s, Kabat-Zinn developed an interest in Buddhist mindfulness techniques and removed them from their religious context and associated rituals.

According to Christophe André, there are three fundamental attitudes that encourage mindfulness: keeping the field of attention as wide as possible, letting go of judgment and control, and being able to observe and feel.

To make mindfulness easier, ideally you should stop what you are doing and take a break to connect with yourself and reflect on either the work you have already accomplished or yourself.

The importance of breathing

We take approximately 26 000 breaths per day, and breathing is an automatic, necessary action. But are we actually aware of our breathing? You may have already noticed that when you pay attention to your breathing, your body relaxes.

How can you become aware of your breathing?

Focus on your body and feel all the sensations caused by each breathing "movement": the air in your nose and throat, the movement of your stomach when it fills with air or lets air out, the expansion of your lungs, and so on.

There are a range of breathing techniques that can help your body to relax and help you to improve your concentration.

- **Controlled breathing:** this involves breathing in while counting 1, 2, 3, etc., then counting to the same number when you breathe out. Make sure that you stay relaxed and that your breathing remains regular.
- **Mindfulness of breathing (Ānāpānasati):** this exercise is used in particular in Vipassanā meditation, which originated in India. it involves pausing before each breath In and each breath out, which forces you to pay attention to your inhalation and exhalation.

When you have mastered these breathing exercises, you can move on to abdominal breathing. This involves breathing in through your nose for five seconds and letting your stomach swell. When you breathe out, let the air out of your stomach and suck it in as far as possible. After five breaths, go back to breathing normally.

Acceptance

Acceptance is a key notion in mindfulness. This does not mean remaining inactive or passive when facing a difficult or unpleasant situation, but rather accepting the way things are without dwelling on the past or letting yourself be overwhelmed by negative thoughts. Accepting your feelings and emotions when dealing with certain events in life is essential, as this will help you to stop resisting the inevitable and therefore reduce the pain these events cause you.

This does not mean that you cannot take action to change things. On the contrary, accepting the situation will make you better able to change it or find a solution because you will no longer by "contaminated" by intrusive thoughts.

Observing your thoughts and emotions

The Vietnamese Buddhist monk Thich Nhat Hanh (born in 1926) suggests a five-step technique to calm your mind and live in the moment. It can be applied to any emotion (anger, sadness, fear, anxiety, etc.).

- **Recognise the emotion.** Realise that you are angry, sad, etc.
- **Accept the emotion.** Accept that this emotion is present in you.
- **Embrace the emotion.** Do not try to fight it or run away from it.
- **Look closely at the emotion.** Observe the emotion closely in order to determine where it came from and what caused it.
- **Understand the emotion.** What was your state of mind when the situation transpired?

When you feel an emotion mounting in you, whether it is anger or sadness, do not simply observe it, but describe it. Rather than simply thinking "I am angry", think "This situation is making me angry" or "I can feel anger rising in me". This allows you to separate yourself from your emotion.

You are not your anger or sadness: your emotions exist within you, but they do not define you. This exercise will also enable you to put your emotions into perspective and observe them more effectively.

MINDFULNESS MEDITATION

PREPARING FOR MINDFULNESS MEDITATION

Before you practise mindfulness meditation, it is worth mastering certain basic skills, and preparing well will make things easier for you. For example, if you already practise another kind of meditation, mindfulness meditation will come more easily to you. However, remember that anyone can meditate, whether or not they have done it before.

- It is very important to **make yourself comfortable** and to choose a calm place, as this will help you to concentrate. You should also think about switching off your phone and moving (or hiding) any objects that could distract you while you are meditating.
- Your posture plays an important role in effective meditation. A balanced body position will make it easier to attain mental balance. If you

find that the seated meditation position does not work for you, you can also lay down on your back.

- Meditating regularly and at a set time will make it easier to get in the right mindset.
- Meditation or yoga classes can also help to make mindfulness meditation automatic to you.
- The best way of avoiding thinking about the time and clockwatching to see how much time you have left is to **set an alarm**. This will allow you to stay completely focused on meditation until the alarm goes off. Ideally, you should know how long you are going to meditate for before you start. Start with five to ten minutes, and increase the time once you feel more comfortable with the exercise.
- **Use smartphone apps.** There are a range of iOS and Android apps in different languages that can help you to meditate. Some of the most popular of these include Imagine Clarity, The Mindfulness App and Headspace.

MINDFULNESS MEDITATION TECHNIQUES

- **Meditation while walking.** The aim of this movement-based meditation is to be completely aware of and present in your movement. Do not set yourself a particular goal, but focus exclusively on walking, your movements, your breathing, your steps, the sensations you feel, and so on.

- **Practise mindfulness while doing housework (washing up, dusting, etc.).** Pay attention to every gesture and, above all, focus so that you are fully aware of what you are doing. Concentrate on your breathing and drive away any intrusive thoughts so that your attention is fully focused on the activity you are doing.

- **Empathetic joy meditation.** Get into the basic meditation position (legs crossed with each foot on the opposite thigh, neck and back straight, hands touching knees, knees on the floor). Once you are mentally relaxed, think about a loved one who is happy and joyful. Think about their presence, their voice and their laughter. Then think about someone who recently had a great experience (for example, a friend who has had a baby, a friend who has got married, a loved one who has received a promotion) and focus on the memory of this happiness. Next, think about someone whom you admire and remind yourself how lucky you are to know them. Finally, turn your attention to yourself: think about your qualities, what you have accomplished, any events that have inspired you, and happy times in your life. Let joy and gratitude wash over you.

- **Meditation about a parent.** This exercise can be tricky, especially if you have had problems with one or both of your parents or if you still frequently clash with them. Get into the basic meditation position and wait for your mind to clear. Focus on either your mother or your father. Imagine them when they were younger: what was their childhood like? What did they look like when they were younger? What were their teenage years like? What were their passions? Next, imagine meeting them at this age. Try to imagine the first years of your childhood through their eyes, and reflect on what they felt and what they struggled with during the different events you have been through together. Let yourself be filled with love and compassion for them.

- **Benevolent love meditation.** This mediation technique has existed for thousands of years. Get into the basic meditation position and start the exercise once your mind has cleared. Repeat the following phrases (or variations on them): "Let me be healthy", "Let me be happy", "Let me be free from suffering". Let yourself be flooded with kindness towards yourself. The first few times you try the exercise, you may have to repeat it before you feel anything. Once you feel the kindness washing over you, repeat the exercise with someone you care about ("Let them be healthy", "Let them be happy", and so on). Next, repeat the exercise with somebody you are indifferent to, and finally with someone you dislike or with whom you have a difficult relationship. If you have completed the first exercises successfully, it will be easier for you to feel compassion towards the person with whom you get on less well.
- **Mentally travelling to different places.**
  - After paying attention to your breathing, direct your thoughts to different places, starting with a part of your body (your left

foot or your right hand, for example). Next, bring your attention back to your breathing before "visiting" another part of your body, such as your right eye or your navel.

- Focus on your breathing again, and then "travel" to the top of the Rockefeller Center in New York. Pay attention to what you feel when your thoughts are there.
- Bring your attention back to your breathing before moving your mind to the Sahara Desert. Focus on what you feel.
- After focusing on your breathing again, mentally travel to the Icelandic glaciers and concentrate on what you feel there.

Pull your mind back to the room you are in and analyse your observations. What did you feel in the different places your thoughts travelled to? This exercise typically shows that we can only focus on a single thought at once, that our thoughts can take us anywhere and, above all, that each thought is connected to a precise feeling. If we think about a place that is associated with happy memories, we will be flooded with happiness. Conversely, if we remember a journey that went badly, an argument or a sad event, we will feel nostalgic or even depressed.

- **Mindful eating.** Eat something as though you are eating it for the first time. For example, imagine that there are no nectarines in your country, so you have never eaten or even seen one. Imagine that you are a tourist, start cutting the nectarine into slices and discover the taste of the fruit and how it feels in your mouth. Examine each slice of the nectarine, smell it and pay attention to the texture of its skin. What sound does it make when you bite into it? Does the taste change while you chew it? This exercise will help you to appreciate the present moment and to rediscover the sensations that you lose with habit and the repetition of everyday gestures.
- **Body scan.** This exercise involves concentrating on the different parts of your body, one after the other. The important thing is the attention that you pay to each body part. It is most common to work from the top to the bottom of the body: head, face, neck, back, chest, stomach, legs, feet, toes. Start by sitting or lying down comfortably. Begin with your head and work through each part: hair, fore-

head, eyes, cheeks, nose, lips, chin, etc. Make sure you take the time to focus on each part before moving on to the next one. The goal of the exercise is to encourage concentration.

TIPS AND TRICKS

- **Write.** Keep a journal of your feelings and thoughts both during your mindfulness meditation and throughout the day. Noting the emotions you felt throughout the day will help you to understand your reactions and give you the perspective you need to achieve mindfulness the next time round.
- **Focus on no more than three exercises at once and work on them for two months.** Once they have become second nature to you, you can incorporate new exercises into your repertoire. For example, you could choose:
  - a breathing exercise;
  - mindfulness while doing the housework;
  - mindful eating.

  Once you have mastered these three exercises, you can try others and work on different breathing techniques.

- **The "pause" button.** Imagine that you have a "pause" button that you can press every time a situation calls for an emotional response. Stopping for a few seconds will allow you to quickly regain control of your emotions. Pressing the "pause" button is easy: simply take a few deep breaths in and out.

INCORPORATING MINDFULNESS INTO YOUR EVERYDAY LIFE

You can practise mindfulness meditation as part of your everyday life, and working on it regularly will enable you to cultivate a state of mindfulness. This will in turn have a positive impact on your relationships with other people.

- When you are in a queue, instead of reaching for your phone and checking your emails or scrolling through social media, concentrate on your breathing and pay attention to the physical sensations you are experiencing.
- Whether you are with your family or with colleagues, give the person you are speaking to your undivided attention. Focus on what they are saying, maintain eye contact, do not interrupt them and pay attention to your body language, as this will help to convey your open-mindedness.
- Start thinking about other people as soon

as you wake up. Think immediately about a person you are going to see today, ask yourself what they might be going through right now, prepare to ask them how they are and how any of their ongoing projects are going, and so on. This will help with your empathetic joy meditation and your benevolent love meditation.

- When conflict arises between you and someone else, try to separate them from the role they represent (your mother, your best friend, your boss, etc.) and see them as another human being. Try to remember that they experience the same emotions, suffering and fears as you. This will enable you to understand them better, view things more calmly and manage the situation better.

OTHER TECHNIQUES

Sophrology

Sophrology is the science of the consciousness in harmony and encompasses a range of practices, including hypnosis, phenomenology, yoga, Buddhism and relaxation. Sophrology aims to use different exercises to develop mindfulness and improve the person's quality of life. It is based on four key principles: listening to the body, stress management, self-confidence and life values. The exercises associated with sophrology are used to broaden the individual's field of consciousness.

Yoga

Yoga is "a type of exercise in which you move your body into various positions in order to become more fit or flexible, to improve your breathing, and to relax your mind". It involves "exercises and postures designed to promote physical and spiritual wellbeing" (*Collins English Dictionary*).

Yoga sessions of all disciplines incorporate mindfulness activities. Elements of yoga have been incorporated into a number of martial arts, Tai Chi, Pilates, qigong, etc.

Slow life

This movement was founded in 1980 by the Italian sociologist Carlo Petrini (born in 1949). Its aim is to allow us to reconnect with our essential, fundamental values and to live life at a slower pace so that we can listen to our minds and bodies, connect with other people, eat better, and so on. According to Cindy Chapelle, who has written a book on the phenomenon, it allows us to put a stop to our frenetic activity in order to bring our attention back to the essentials, live in the moment and thrive (2016). This slower pace of life allows us to become more attuned to our surroundings and what is happening in our lives.

FAQS

IS MEDITATION ABSOLUTELY NECESSARY TO ACHIEVE MINDFULNESS?

No: mindfulness is not linked to meditation as such, and there are ways of practising mindfulness without meditating. For example, Acceptance and Commitment Therapy (ACT) advocates practising mindfulness independently of meditation.

ACT is based on four psychological skills that help individuals to attain mindfulness:

- cognitive defusion, which allows them to put things in perspective and let their thoughts go by;
- acceptance, which allows them to let go of painful feelings;
- contact with the present moment;
- the observing self, which allows them to access a transcendent sense of self.

Another method involves remaining aware of all the things that we normally do automatically: brushing our teeth, showering, eating breakfast, and so on. It involves paying particular attention to these gestures and to our feelings when we carry them out.

HOW MUCH TIME SHOULD I DEDICATE TO PRACTISING MINDFULNESS?

The most important thing is not how much time we spend practising mindfulness meditation, but rather how often and how regularly we do it. To make progress with meditation, it is advised to mediate for at least five to ten minutes every day.

Decide on a length of time to set aside for meditation, a time of day to do it and an appropriate frequency. If you decided to meditate for five minutes per day (in the morning when you wake up, for example), you must stick to it and make meditation part of your morning routine. Meditating at the same time every day will make it easier to turn it into a habit. If you are too ambitious or set the bar too high to begin with, you risk not sticking to it.

Of course, the amount of time you devote to mindfulness meditation will depend on your needs, so it is up to you to find out what works for you.

HOW CAN I USE MINDFULNESS TO RESOLVE CONFLICTS?

As you practise mindfulness, you will learn to better manage your emotions, put complicated situations into perspective, observe your thoughts and accept your emotions. This means that you will be able to avoid conflicts more easily.

When they do arise, facing up to your thoughts and emotions and being fully aware of them will help you to emerge from the conflict with a smile.

WHAT ARE THE BENEFITS OF MINDFULNESS?

Mindfulness has many benefits. Among others, it helps us to develop our emotional intelligence as it increases our awareness of our own emotions and enables us to better understand other people's emotions. It also helps us to become calmer and to deal with problems differently, as practising mindfulness makes it easier to put our issues into perspective.

WHAT ARE THE LINKS BETWEEN SLOW LIFE AND MINDFULNESS?

Slow life is the art of slowing down our pace of life in order to make the most of life's little pleasures. Practising mindfulness can help us to master slow life. Listening to our body allows us to slow down, while mindful eating allows us to savour tastes and is clearly linked to slow food. Mindfulness also enables us to better recognise our emotions and increase our self-awareness. This is an important part of slow life, which aims to help us to live in accordance with our values. Finally, mindfulness allows us to better manage stress and therefore to act more calmly.

DO I HAVE TO BE AN EXPERT IN SPIRITUALITY TO MEDITATE?

There are a number of misconceptions surrounding mediation, many of which are linked to Buddhism. However, meditation is not just a religious or spiritual activity, and its aim is not only to empty our minds. In fact, it is accessible to everyone, as long as they work at it. This means that there is no need to be an expert in spirituality or to convert to Buddhism to practise meditation successfully!

WHAT SHOULD I DO WHEN MY THOUGHTS GET IN THE WAY OF MINDFULNESS?

Often (and especially when we are just starting out), intrusive thoughts keep popping into our heads, making it difficult or impossible to achieve mindfulness. In this case, you need to know the steps to follow to stop your thoughts from overwhelming you.

• Do not feel guilty or get angry with yourself

for letting these thoughts reach you.

- Always keep a notebook and pen or pencil within reach. This will allow you to write your thoughts down and be rid of them more quickly.
- Focus on a detail (your breathing, the ticking of the clock, the hem of your clothing, etc.) in order to redirect your attention.
- Let go of these thoughts and let them pass you by.

FURTHER READING

BIBLIOGRAPHY

- André, C. (2010) La méditation en pleine conscience. *Cerveau&Psycho*. (41). pp. 18-21.

- Baert, S. (2015) 3 exercices pour débuter la méditation en pleine conscience. *Mon Coach de Relaxation*. [Online]. [Accessed 21 November 2017]. Available from: <https://moncoachderelaxation.com/exercices-meditation/>

- Brown, K. W. and Ryan, R. M. (No date) Mindful Attention Awareness Scale. *Journal of Personality and Social Psychology*. [Online]. [Accessed 21 November 2017]. Available from: <https://ppc.sas.upenn.edu/resources/questionnaires-researchers/mindful-attention-awareness-scale>

- Chapelle, C. (2016) *La slow life en pleine conscience*. Saint-Julien-en-Genevois: Éditions Jouvence.

- Descheneaux, N. (No date) La méditation pleine conscience, comment et pourquoi la pratiquer. *Canal Vie*. [Online]. [Accessed 21 November 2017]. Available from: <http://www.canalvie.com/sante-beaute/bien-etre/meditation-pleine-conscience-1.1687849>

- Doyle, O. (2014) *Mindfulness Plain & Simple.* London: Orion Publishing Group.

- Harris, R. (2009) Mindfulness without meditation. *Healthcare Counselling & Psychotherapy.* pp. 21-24.

- Killingsworth, M. A. and Gilbert, D. T. (2010) A Wandering Mind is an Unhappy Mind. *Harvard Gazette.* [Online]. [Accessed 21 November 2017]. Available from: <https://news.harvard.edu/gazette/story/2010/11/wandering-mind-not-a-happy-mind/>

- Psychomédie (2013) *Pleine conscience : 4 exercises pour s'initier.* [Online]. [Accessed 21 November 2017]. Available from: <http://www.psychomedia.qc.ca/psychologie/2013-12-26/exercice-initiation-a-la-pleine-conscience-mindfulness>

- Von Hehn, S. and Von Hehn, A. (2015) *La pleine conscience. Apprendre à méditer au quotidien !* Brussels: Ixelles Éditions.

ADDITIONAL SOURCES

- Chaskalson, M. (2014) *Mindfulness in Eight Weeks: The revolutionary 8 week plan to clear your mind and calm your life.* London: HarperThorsons.

- Gunaratana, H. (1991) *Mindfulness.* Taipei: The Corporate Body of the Buddha Educational Foundation.

- Sweet, C. and Mihotich, M. (2014) *The Mindfulness*

Journal: Exercises to help you find peace and calm wherever you are. London: Boxtree.

- Williams, M. and Penman, D. (2011) *Mindfulness: A practical guide to finding peace in a frantic world.* London: Piatkus.

50MINUTES.com

IMPROVE YOUR GENERAL KNOWLEDGE

IN A BLINK OF AN EYE !

www.50minutes.com